Imagine That!
31 Days of Purpose Filled Analogies

Written By Sherry Pitts

Imagine That
31 Days of Purpose Filled Analogies

Copyright © 2018 Sherry Pitts

All rights reserved. In accordance with the U.S. Copyright Act of 1976, the scanning, uploading and electronic sharing of any part of this book without the written permission of the publisher constitutes unlawful piracy and theft of the author's intellectual property. For permission to use material from this book; other than for review purposes, prior written permission must be obtained by contacting the author at SPittsImagineThat@gmail.com.

ISBN: 978-1987478914

About the Author

Sherry Pitts was born Sherry Turner in Dayton, Ohio to Abraham Sr. and Lula Turner. She is a graduate of Wilberforce University, where she earned a Bachelor's Degree in Organizational Management. As a mother of six children, and two grandchildren, Sherry believes education is the key to unlocking every child's greatest potential. She remains a strong advocate for educational options for minority and disadvantaged youth. She has served with memberships to such organizations as Black Alliance for Educational Options (BAEO) and Parents Advancing Choice in Education (P.A.C.E). Sherry currently works as a Special Assistant to the founder and president of Campaign for School Equity, which is an organization that empowers and equips youth, parents, and communities with the tools, education, and information to better navigate their educational choices. She is a faithful Christian and the wife of *Virgil Pitts. She has been married for 29 years.*

Sherry is an active member of Bates Memorial Baptist Church in Louisville, KY under the pastoral leadership of Dr. F. Bruce Williams. She has participated in choir, assimilation ministry, and other programs. Through Sherry's regular attendance in hearing God's word, participating in church functions and studying God's word, God began to reveal His purpose for her life; to humbly serve God while inspiring people through prayer and encouragement to achieve their destiny.

The author is known among her friends and family as a person who provides analogies to paint a picture of their topic of discussion. Sherry learned, later in life, that she is a visual learner. Although she was unaware of this type of learning style when she was younger, she has embraced it and uses it to teach others how to "see" their situation through mental pictures.

Sherry is full of inspiring and encouraging words. She finds the good in any situation and lights up a room with her sunny personality. Sherry has a heart for God, thus the reason she has such a big heart for people.

This book is dedicated to:

My six children Christopher, Stanley, Natalie, Charity, Macy and Trinity. My two grandchildren, Nia and Carter for their love, respect and honor for me.

To my mother and father Abraham Sr. and Lula Turner for teaching me about God at an early age and being the example of a loving faithful couple for over 60 years. For ALWAYS seeing the best in me even when my faults were great.

To my brothers and sisters, Abraham Turner Jr., Sandra Kitwana, Felix Turner and Angela Dago for supporting, embracing and showing me what family is all about through your giving of time, resources and more importantly your love.

And finally, to my husband, Virgil Pitts, for all your care, trust, belief in me, love for me and, most importantly, for being my spiritual covering.

Table of Contents

Day 1: Umbrella - *A Wife's Covering is Her Husband*

Day 2: Lamp - *See Clearly*

Day 3: Dropped Wallet - *Giving*

Day 4: Vegetables - *The Gift of Sharing*

Day 5: The Car - *Moving with God*

Day 6: Lost Bracelet - *Seek and You Shall Find*

Day 7: Hurricane - *The Power of Planning*

Day 8: The Blender - *The Right Connection*

Day 9: Palm Tree - *Bend, Don't Break*

Day 10: Baseball Catcher - *Ready to Receive*

Day 11: The Gift - *Being Thankful*

Day 12: Itchy Back - *Depending on Others*

Day 13: The Mailman - *What's in the Mail?*

Day 14: Laundry - *Spiritual Cleansing*

Day 15: GPS - *Finding your Way*

Day 16: Television - *Turn it On*

Day 17: Piggy Bank - *Knowing Your Worth*

Day 18: The Eulogy - *Be the Change God Wants You to Be*

Day 19: Shoes - *Working in Your Gifts and Talents*

Day 20: Coffee Pot - *Reading the Instructions*

Day 21: Key to Ignition - *Exercising Your Faith*

Day 22: Student and the Teacher - *Spiritual Partner*

Day 23: Dandelion - *Cutting the Root*

Day 24: Heart Monitor - *Trials and Tribulations*

Day 25: Stepping Stone - *Guidance in a Storm*

Day 26: Seed - *Spirit of Expectation*

Day 27: Muscle Up! - *Strong Faith*

Day 28: Restaurant Cup - *Getting Filled with the Fullness of God*

Day 29: Sun - *God is Here*

Day 30: Surge Protector - *Overflow of Blessings*

Day 31: We are the Writers; God is the Editor

Foreword

Every answer we need can be found in God's Word. Some answers are not literal, but if we are careful to study the Bible and apply it to our lives we have everything we could possibly need. The Bible says, "Your word is a lamp for my feet and light to my path." This scripture (Psalm 119:105) tells us that God's Word can guide our every step and lead us wherever we are to go. Imagine That!

In this power packed devotional, Sherry Ann Pitts paints a clear picture of how to allow God's Word to be a lamp for our feet and a light to our path. Sherry shares real life situations and practical examples from her own experiences. Her delivery is clothed in humility and doused in love. In each devotion, Sherry shows us how so often we miss messages from God and answers to prayer because we are looking for grandiose experiences. We are expecting the heavens to literally open and Jesus to step down into our bedroom to speak to us. God has provided His Word and the Holy Spirit to guide us and lead us. The answers we need are often simple and subtle. We must simply be sensitive enough to not miss the message or answer to our prayer.

My name is Tanya DeFreitas. I am a wife, a mother, an entrepreneur, an author, and a motivational speaker. For me, life stays busy and in the midst of the busyness it is critical to be able to hear from God. Sometimes I miss the message or I overlook the answer, yet I am learning daily. In fact, the start of my friendship with Sherry was an answer to prayer. Had I not been sensitive to the Holy Spirit, I would have missed the leading of God.

Sherry and I were a part of an authorship program where we both received coaching on completing a manuscript. There were several other writers in the program and I made an effort to engage with all of them. I was prompted however, to reach out to Sherry, personally. While I felt it was God prompting me, I was still hesitant. Ultimately, I knew I had to be obedient.

I sent Sherry a message through Facebook. She was responsive and we clicked immediately. Her personality shined brightly even through a virtual message. We exchanged telephone numbers and that was the beginning of what I believe to be a lifelong friendship.

Proverbs 18:24 says, "A man who has friends must himself be friendly, but there is a friend who sticks closer than a brother." Before connecting with

Sherry, I had recently lost two dear friends. Their season in my life came to an abrupt end and it was a painful experience. I was not in need of new friends per say, however, I had cried out to God about the pain I felt over the loss. I had thought those two friendships would never end. I considered those two friends to be like family. God knew my heart. God knew Sherry's heart. I didn't. He knew Sherry's future and mine. He also knew that we would be vital to helping one another grow as women in faith and to leap into our destiny. Had I missed the opportunity, I may have missed the many blessings shared between Sherry and I. Imagine That!

As you read the forthcoming devotions, be open and receptive to the prompting of the Holy Spirit. You will begin to hear and see your own experiences of how God uses His Word to lead and guide us. You will begin to identify the simple and subtle ways in which God communicates with you daily and moment by moment. Listen carefully to Sherry's examples as God uses her to show you messages in everyday life. I assure you everything that you need is in God's Word and every answer you seek has already been provided. Can you imagine that?

Blessings to you,

T. DeFreitas

The Umbrella

A Wife's Covering is Her Husband

"Husbands, love your wives, even as Christ also loved the church, and gave Himself for it...Ephesians 5:25"

A wife's covering is her husband, the "umbrella". When it rains outside, as long as she is under the umbrella she is covered. She can see the rain, but it doesn't touch her. But, if she steps from under the umbrella, the rain will fall on her. She can feel the elements now. To keep her covering she must stay under the umbrella (covering). The umbrella will sustain tears (temptation) every now and then and may even experience a rip. The umbrella is still trying to protect what is under it. Often it doesn't realize it has a rip or even how big it has become. The wife can see the rip and it is her job (the helpmate) to pray (place a patch over the hole) until the hole can be replaced (renewed in Christ).

Umbrellas come in all shapes and sizes, but they are meant to do one job; keep you covered. The umbrella can't do the work by itself, but has to be opened before it can protect. Wives, we have to open our hearts to our husbands so he can protect us. Husbands have been given an assignment to protect their wives.

On a beautiful sunny day, when the clouds move in and the sun fades away giving way to the rain, it's good to know you have an umbrella. When it's not raining, we tend to take the umbrella for granted. It's not needed when the sun shines, so we think. Too often we forget that when the sun is shining so brightly, that very umbrella can be a shield to those bright rays.

As a husband provides a covering for his wife, be reminded to appreciate the covering (umbrella) and never take it for granted. Even though it's designed to protect you from the rain, it can be used for other purposes. And, when a wife takes care of her umbrella, she should expect for it to provide the necessary covering.

Lamp

See Clearly

"Let your light shine before men so that they will see your good deeds...Matthew 5:16"

A lamp brings light to darkness. Typically, you don't place a lamp in the sunlight because there is light there already. A lamp is most useful when darkness approaches or it is dark. As Christians, God often places us in dark situations to bring (light) awareness to others. I've heard some Christians say, "Why am I around all these negative people?" Or, "Why do I have to work such a terrible job?" Have you ever considered God has you where He needs you not for your benefit but for someone else's? Have you ever considered that God has given you something for the sole purpose of giving it away? Being positioned as an obedient Christian is key to the fulfillment of God's promises in other people's lives. There are people who are praying to God and believing that their prayers will come to pass. You might be working in that mortgage department to approve their loan. You might be employed in a school to offer more financial assistance to a family that would not get it without your help. You could be positioned in a wife group to share your testimony of how you made it through a rough patch in your marriage. God will shine His light through you.

    The lamp by itself cannot be turned on. It takes the effort of the believer to trust that when we flip the switch, light will come on. When we purchase the lamp, we don't give consideration to the components of the lamp. We've seen how lamps work and we know that when you plug it into a power source it turns on. We don't know how God works but we know when we pray, and stay connected, He works it out. He is our power source. In our natural minds, we can't see how it works, but we know that our belief and trust in God ignites our faith and we know that it will work.

When a person turns on the light and it does not come on, typically he doesn't say, "Oh, the light won't come on". He checks to see if it is plugged in, or if the light bulb is out, etc. Why? Because there is an expectation that the light is supposed to turn on because we've seen it happen before. This is our faith at work. If we go to God asking in prayer this is His promise, *"Whatever you ask for in prayer, believe that you have received it, and it will be yours."*

When we don't receive, we should begin to check ourselves. Are we in God's will? Do we stand believing that we will receive what we are asking from God? Does it align with God's purpose for our lives? After careful consideration, should this lamp turn on? As we look into (search) our hearts and seek God's word we tend to find why the lamp is not coming on. *"Examine yourselves to see whether you are in the faith."*

Are you being the light God wants you to be? Are you being a light that blesses others? Or, are you experiencing a power failure?

Dropped Wallet

Giving

"Give, and it will be given to you. A good measure, pressed down, shaken together and running over, will be poured into your lap. For with the measure you use, it will be measured to you...Luke 6:38"

My daughter dropped her wallet in the parking lot of a well-known drugstore. Before she entered the store, a gentleman who appeared to be homeless greeted her. She smiled and said hello, however, as she returned to her car she realized she misplaced her wallet. After looking around in her car and in her bags, she got out of her car to re-trace her steps. As she began searching she saw the homeless gentleman pick up the wallet. They looked at each other and he ran away with the wallet! As my daughter stood in amazement that he took her wallet, she quickly thought, "I hope he does something good with the money. I would have given him more if only he had given it back to me". Not only was her money in the wallet, but her driver's license, and other credentials. Those items were of value to her, so giving him the money to say thank you would have been his reward, without the guilt of taking something that did not belong to him.

You see, the gentleman saw an opportunity in the moment. What he didn't know, was that there was a reward (blessing) in the giving. If he had given the wallet (his life) to the owner (God), the reward would have been great. Peace, inner joy, contentment are a few of those rewards. These rewards (blessings) cannot be bought they only come from God. We often find ourselves taking what we see as an opportunity for our gain, especially in the workplace, when really we are backstabbing, cheating and stealing just to get ahead. Those are stolen opportunities. We settle for the crumbs when God wants to invite us to the table.

Could you trust God to provide for you if you found a wallet full of money and you needed what was in that wallet?

Vegetables

The Gift of Sharing

"And do not forget to do good and share with others, for with such sacrifices God is pleased...Hebrews 13:16"

    I've heard so many children say, "I don't like my peas, or carrots, or green beans" (laughter). There's something about fresh vegetables (gifts). We either dislike or embrace them. They are good for us; they have a beauty about them with their different colors and textures. When we receive fresh vegetables (gifts/talents) we store them in our refrigerator (heart) to preserve them. However, the vegetables are never meant to stay in the refrigerator. They are meant to be consumed. When we consume the vegetables, they become part of us and are good for our whole body. In return, we are good for those around us. Our being is wholesome. When we consume that which is good, it makes us a well-rounded person, which enables us to be a blessing. God blesses each one of us with gifts and talents. When we don't use them, we could lose them.

There have been times that I've cleaned my refrigerator and noticed the lettuce has withered, or the celery was no longer crisp. I had to throw them out. If only I had used those vegetables, or given them (shared my gifts/talents) to someone, they would not have been wasted. How many times have we received good vegetables, put them in the refrigerator and watched them wither away?

Are you using your gifts/talents? Have your talents been stored and forgotten?

It should be our goal, as Christians, to do good, share our time, talents, resources, and most of all God's word, with others. God gives us gifts and blessings not to keep to ourselves, but to give to others.

The Car

Moving with God

> *"But those who hope in the Lord will renew their strength. They will soar on wings like eagles; they will run and not grow weary, they will walk and not be faint...Isaiah 40:31"*

Cars today can accelerate up to 120 miles per hour and even faster. If you have a standard car with a stick shift you know about gears and how they can slip. If you don't engage everything correctly, the gears in the transmission can slip. Once that happens, your car will only go so fast because it is stuck in a lower gear.

The ups and downs of life can weigh heavy on a person's mind and cause him or her to get stuck in thought. This process tends to hold a person in the low gear of their life just when they are about to receive a breakthrough.

Driving on the highway requires us to drive at a higher speed limit. Have you ever driven on the highway and ended up behind someone driving 30 miles under the speed limit? Have you ever wondered why some people seem to go so slow when they're in the fast lane? In your mind you're screaming at them to get over and let everyone pass!

Situations in life can cause us to live and think at 40 miles per hour when God wants us to accelerate to 70 miles per hour. Our car is capable of performing at that speed, but we won't accelerate.

God wants us to prosper. He has given us a car that can reach speeds of over 120 miles per hour. We may find ourselves talking to our friends, family and church associates, asking the question, "Why am I stuck in this situation?" We have the transportation to take us to the next level, but we have to be willing to put the car in the right gear to get the maximum speed. We have to do the work.

The gear shaft is there, we have to grab it and move it to the desired gear.

Do we need to drive slowly in low gear to get out of a sticky situation? Do we need to stay neutral and hear from God? Do we need to park and be still? Or, do we need to put our faith in drive and accelerate onto the highway and get what God has for us? When we pray God hears us. He will instruct us. We have to be willing to do the work and move the gear. Faith without works is dead. We are given choices.

When you pray are you listening for God's answer? Are you willing to move when God gives the command? What gear are you in right now?

Lost Bracelet

Seek and You Shall Find

"For the Son of man came to seek and save the lost...Luke 19:10"

    I believe in giving a person their flowers while they live. I had a favorite bracelet that I gave to my daughter, Charity, so she could enjoy it now. Before I gave Charity the bracelet, I expressed how important it was to me and that I wanted her to have it. Charity was very excited. She said she would cherish and take great care of it.

    A year later Charity attended a friend's party and she decided to wear the bracelet. When she got home from the party she realized the bracelet was not on her wrist. Her heart began racing. Thoughts of its value, both to her and I, consumed her mind.

    Charity called me with worry in her voice and told me she had lost the bracelet. She called her friend several times to inquire if she found the bracelet in her apartment. Her friend told her no, she had not found it. Her friend asked Charity if Charity wanted to come and look as she may be able to backtrack her steps and look for it. When Charity went to her friend's house, she explained how important the bracelet was to her. At that moment, her friend began to search for this "valuable" bracelet. Because they both knew it had value, they searched in earnest. Before long her friend found the bracelet. She had been looking for days, not knowing the worth or value it had. When she shouted, "Charity, I found the bracelet!", they both felt a peace come over them.

    The bracelet could have been replaced, but for Charity it was one-of-a-kind and had meaning. (Thou shall have no other gods before me). She continued to search (seek and you shall find) until she found it. Our God is the same way. Once we accept God in our lives and know the value of His love, mercy and grace, we don't ever want to lose Him. We will seek Him until we find Him.

Hurricane

The Power of Planning

"The foolish ones took their lamps but did not take any oil with them...Matthew 25:3"

I went to the store to get bread, eggs, milk, a blanket, water and a few candles. I'm from a northern state, and was vacationing in Florida at the time. Many of the shelves were bare and people had baskets full of items, lots of items. Ironically, the items I went to purchase were not available. Why were the shelves so empty? Did the store not know about supply and demand? The demand was high and the supplies were low. What I didn't know was that the meteorologists had broadcasted a hurricane was coming.

The citizens of Florida knew what it meant to prepare for a hurricane. They didn't wait until the storm hit land before going to the store. This storm was forecasted to be the mother of all hurricanes.

It would travel and hit every part of Florida and cause major destruction in some areas. There were designated evacuation shelters and some residents decided to leave the area. Living in a northern state, I had never experienced this type of storm so I didn't quite know how to prepare for it, obviously.

    I began to watch the residents. I saw how they prepared. It reminded me of how Christians put on their armor of God. They knew the forces of a hurricane and the destruction it could bring. Christians know the armor of God will enable them to stand their ground through any of life's storms. When the hurricane was forecasted, they went to the stores and acquired the items they needed. They knew what stores stocked the critical supplies: water and candles. Unlike the foolish bridesmaids, stated in Matthew 25:3, that did not take enough oil with them to meet the bridegroom and missed their opportunity because they were not prepared at the appointed time, the people of

Florida stored enough supplies for the appointed time of the hurricane. We, in the same way, should always be prepared for the coming of the Lord. Don't miss your bridegroom and fall prey to the destruction that awaits a soul that is not found to be in Christ!

The Blender

The Right Connection

"Remain in me as I also will remain in you...John 15:4"

Jesus Christ tells us in John 15:4 that if we stay connected to him, he will stay connected to us. I recall a time when I invited a few friends over for smoothies. I went to the store and purchased a new smoothie blender, fruit, yogurt and a few vegetables. At home, I set my table up with cute cups and special straws to sip up the thick smoothies. I had monogram napkins for each of my guests. Oh, it was set up nicely! As my guests arrived, we sat in the living room and talked for a while. We then moved to the kitchen. I asked each guest what type of smoothie she would like. I prepared their ingredients in individual cups to be sure I didn't blend the wrong combinations.

I took the new blender out, added the first set of ingredients, and attempted to plug in the blender cord. I found out my blender had a three-prong connector. I had the perfect setting; my friends were over having a good time, and we were ready to make smoothies. But, I didn't have the right connection. The fruit was fresh, the vegetables were crisp and the yogurt was cold. I had everything needed to make the smoothie but I wasn't connected to the source that would give me power to make the smoothies.

Have you prepared a speech, a sermon or a report and when it was time to present it, there was no power in it? Did you connect to your source (God)? Did you check your connection? We can have all the tools but if we are not connected to the source to give us power to put the tools in operation, you will end up like I did with all the ingredients and no power. It wasn't until I got the adapter and connected to the power source that I was able to produce my smoothies.

When our connection doesn't connect, we shouldn't give up, we should look for the adapter (prayer), and make the connection.

What are you doing right now that will require you to connect to THE POWER?

The Palm Tree

Bend, Don't Break

"The righteous man will flourish like the palm tree; he will grow like a cedar in Lebanon...Psalm 92:12"

The Palm Tree is a beautiful tree. When I look at the Palms, I see a variation of tall and short trees with gorgeous green leaves that wave beautifully in the air as the winds glide upon them.

Those trees have tough exteriors with strong roots to withstand hurricane force winds. When I think about going through tough times, I find myself comparing my strength to the strength of the Palm Tree. Whether the outside elements are rain, a sunny day or strong winds, the Palm Tree endures it all. During the rain, the roots take in the water and nurture the tree. When the sun is shining the beauty and strength of the tree is displayed, and when strong winds come upon the tree, its strength is displayed by standing firm, rooted and grounded. The leaves bend back and forth. At times it almost seems as if they are going to break. Then quickly, I notice, they sway back to their original position. During the storm, this process goes on for a while. When the storm is over and the rain has cleared the beauty of the Palm remains. It's difficult to tell that the leaves were swaying so hard they looked like they were going to snap.

Our lives are so similar. Are we like the Palm Trees? When it rains in our lives and we are up against troubles, do we use the rain as a source of strength? The rain (trouble) is really to make us stronger, but we see it as an inconvenience at times. In actuality, we need the rain to enjoy the sunny days. When trouble comes our way, it will test our faith and cause us to sway back and forth. During this time, we must remember the source of our strength (God). Just as the Palm Tree relies on the strength of the roots and the base of the tree, we rely on God. We are all beautiful and fully equipped to handle the storms that come our way. We have to remember in all our beauty, the rain, storm and sunny days will come. However, we are made to withstand it all as long as we stay rooted in God.

Baseball Catcher

Ready to Receive

"But blessed is the one who trusts in the LORD, whose confidence is in him...Jeremiah 17:7"

Baseball is a fascinating game to me. I've never played the sport, but I've always been intrigued with the catcher's position. When the pitcher throws the ball, the catcher has to be ready to receive it. The catcher has to be positioned just right with the glove open. I've never seen a catcher with his glove closed when the pitcher is throwing the ball. The catcher's position looks easy, but I've heard when you squat and catch a ball at high speeds it can be difficult. It takes balance and lots of practice. I can imagine that the catcher's knees get tired. I've seen them stand up and stretch. However, I've never seen a catcher leave a game because he was tired of squatting. The catcher usually stays in his position until the inning is complete.

Just like the catcher, we have to be ready to receive from God. When God sends blessings our way, our hearts must be open. Too many of us get tired of being in our positions. We tend to move when God is asking us to be still. And, just when we move, we miss the blessing. It is not always easy being in certain positions (the police officer who stands in the rain and directs traffic because the traffic lights are malfunctioning or the parent who works three jobs to make ends meet), but when we are obedient and steadfast, we will eventually catch the ball (blessing). What happens if the police officer moves or the parent stops working? There might be car accidents or children with no home or food. Just like the catcher, if he doesn't catch the ball so many things could go wrong. The other team could advance to the next base or score.

So, we must be consistent to protect those we serve and to be positioned where God wants us to be to receive.

Have you moved from your position? If so, why? If not, what keeps you grounded?

The Gift

Being Thankful

"I will give thanks to you, LORD, with all my heart; I will tell of all your wonderful deeds...Psalm 9:1"

My husband enjoys buying superhero clothes for our 4-year-old grandson, Carter. Our grandchildren call us, Honey and Botty! Those are the names we chose for our grandchildren to call us!

We were in the truck waiting for the school doors to open to take Carter to class. While waiting, Carter said to me, "Honey, Botty always buys me things. He got me Batman, Paw Patrol, and a PJ Mask." I could see my husband smiling with joy in his heart as Carter spoke those words. What Carter didn't realize was the more thanks and acknowledgement he gave his grandfather, the more Virgil wanted to do for Carter. As Carter walked into school, he summoned his teacher to examine his new shirt. "It's Batman!" he exclaimed, "My Botty bought it!" During recess, Carter gathered with his friends and showed them his Paw Patrol gloves. When we picked Carter up from school, he shared with us he didn't lose his Batman hat. He put it in his book bag because he wanted to take care of it.

Carter, at a young age, has a desire to tell those he knows about the gifts he has received. Those who are new Christians enjoy sharing the good works of God. There is an excitement as they speak. There is an expectation that those they tell about the good works of God, will want to know more about Him.

Our Father in heaven wants to bless us. As we acknowledge God and give HIM thanks for the many blessings HE bestows upon us, it delights Him and the blessings continue to flow. I have witnessed many people receiving from others with an ungrateful heart, or a spirit of entitlement. God loves a cheerful giver, and He exemplifies His expectation by giving us grace and mercy every day.

Do you give out of obligation or from a giving spirit? How often do you thank those who bless you?

Itchy Back

Depending on Others

"As iron sharpens iron, so one person sharpens another...Proverbs 27:17"

What do you do when your forearm itches? Most of us use the hand of the other arm to scratch it. What about that itch on your nose? Of course, we reach up with our hand and give it a couple of scratches to relieve the itch. How relieved it feels afterwards. When we are able to reach an area on our body to scratch, we normally don't think about it, we automatically take care of it. Have you ever had an itch on your back that you couldn't reach? What do you do?

Our bodies are equipped to scratch those itchy spots. We have nails on our hands to dig into those irritating spots and give ourselves relief. So, why can't we scratch our backs?

God never intended for us to live alone or be alone. We can do most things by ourselves, but there are some things we have to depend on others to do for us. Knowing there is someone you can depend on to scratch your back is comforting. Most people will not ask a stranger to scratch their back. After all, you have to expose your back to get the true effect of the scratch.

God is our personal friend. He is always ready to help us in a time of need. As we live, we will find ourselves in situations that need the help of a friend, more importantly the help of God. Just as we need someone to help us, there will be people surrounding you that will need your help.

Have you positioned yourself to be a friend? How do you ask for help in a time of need?

The Mailman

What's in the Mail?

"Give and it will be given to you...Luke 6:38"

Our mailmen/mailwomen are dedicated servants and I thank God for them. They deliver our mail in the rain, sleet, snow, sunshine and every other kind of element. They have delivered checks, bills, love letters, coupons, etc. While sorting mail on a regular basis, they probably know when a check, gas and light bill or a booklet of coupons is in an envelope. The job of the mailman is to deliver the mail. It's not their job to assume how much is in the check or how much the coupons are worth. The government entrusts the mailman to treat every piece of mail as if it were very important. They take the mail to the customers without opening any of the items.

God may have placed you in a mailman's role. Have you ever been moved to bless someone with a few dollars, call someone to pray for them, or offer to watch your friend's children? You have been called to deliver a blessing. There are times when we are strategically placed so God can use us. We don't need to know what a person has need of. We just need to pray. We don't need to know how much money is needed. We just need to give. We don't need to know why our friends need a break from their children. We just need to be there to help. Don't get me wrong, there are times when we need to know specifics, but when God calls us to "deliver" a message or give, we need to be obedient in following His word. God will not put on us more than we can bear. God is specific. As a willing servant (mailman) He moves on us to do His work. Just like the mailman goes out for his deliveries but does not concern himself with the content of the mail, we should also be ready and prepared to be a blessing to someone no matter their situation.

Has God placed it on your heart to call someone that really needed the encouragement? Have you given someone money only to find out they desperately needed that very amount?

Laundry

Spiritual Cleansing

"If we confess our sins, he is faithful and just to forgive us our sins and to cleanse us from all unrighteousness. 1 John 1:9"

I enjoy doing laundry because it reminds me of the spiritual process we go through. When we purchase a new outfit, there is excitement about when we will wear it. The outfit is clean without any blemishes. After we wear the outfit, there will come a time when we will have to launder it. We are careful to wash it in the right temperature and with the right detergent. After the outfit is washed, it goes in the dryer. When this cycle is complete, the outfit is ready to wear again.

When we accept Christ in our hearts, we are made new. As we live our lives, because we are not perfect beings, we often fall into sin. That is like the new outfit getting dirty. We go before God and ask for forgiveness. We are washed and cleansed, and sometimes we may have to go through the fire (the dryer). After we go through our forgiveness process, we are ready to live a sin free life. We can wear some of our outfits several times before we clean them, but soon, it must go through the launder stage. Our spiritual lives go through a laundering stage also. As we dip in sin, we find ourselves needing to go before God to be washed and cleansed.

There are some outfits we don't wear as often because we know the value of them. We don't have to launder them too often. We take better care of them. Our spiritual lives should be the same way.

How often do you ask for forgiveness? Is it something you could have prevented? Do you try to avoid the same sin? If so, how? If not, what gives you strength to not commit the same sin?

GPS (God Positioning his Saints)

Finding Your Way

"In all your ways submit to him, and he will make your paths straight...Proverbs 3:6"

Road trips are great! Have you ever ventured out with determination to have a good time and your mapping technology to guide you? My family and I were en route to Danville, KY to attend our son's basketball game. We believe in supporting our children and have driven to many unknown places. We didn't know exactly where the stadium was located, but we had a general idea of the main roads and the area. My husband entered the address into the mapping technology and off we went. Some of the roads didn't have street names, just the routes or highway numbers. Our mapping technology got a little confused and began leading us to streets that didn't exist. We drove into someone's backyard and encountered cattle by our vehicle. I was startled beyond words but my husband thought the best way to get out of there was to continue to drive. It seemed as though we were driving in circles.

Finally, my husband stopped and reprogrammed his mind and called upon the GPS (God Positioning his Saints). My husband began to pray. He applied scripture to our situation. *Psalm 143:8 Let the morning bring me word of your unfailing love, for I have put my trust in you. Show me the way I should go, for to you I entrust my life.* After praying, my husband was led to turn down certain roads. He made a left here and a right there. Eventually we were back on the main road.

Technology is wonderful, but when it fails, there is a GPS (God Positioning his Saints) we can call on. When you know the word of God, you can apply His word to your circumstance. There will be times when people will fail us, cell phone batteries will die and mapping technology will give you the wrong directions. As long as you can call on God, His direction will always lead you in the right path.

Television

Turn It On

"Where there is no vision...Proverbs 29:18"

Most households have televisions in at least one room. With cable and local channels, there are so many television programs to watch. When I look at my television, all I see is a black screen. I know there are shows to watch, but I can't hear a sound. There is no picture on the television, just a blank screen. I have a remote control to the television and batteries to go with it. The television is hooked up, but still no picture. Oh, I have to turn it on!

Life sometimes is like a television that is not turned on. God has equipped us with knowledge and ideas, but we find ourselves not tapping into it. We don't turn on the television within us so we can receive all that God has for us. We know what's inside of us but having the courage to turn ourselves on to explore what God has placed in us is often a challenge. The cable channels offer so many programs. There is a channel guide to give a brief summary about each show to help you determine if you want to watch the show. God gives us the same courtesy in our lives. God will give us guidance about our goals, visions, and dreams. God gives us a preview of our lives through our visions.

There are so many ideas within us. Throughout the day we are exposed to creative mental impressions. These are our gifts from God. When we get the courage to tap into our natural ability all the channels become visible. It's nice to have access to all the channels of your television and you decide what you will watch. So, this time as I sit before my television I will use the remote to turn the television on. I will observe each channel through the guide as I decide which show to watch. And in Christ, I will open my heart while listening for God to guide me in my gifts.

Piggy Bank

Knowing Your Worth

"Because you are precious in my eyes...Isaiah 43:4"

As a young girl I would look for pennies to put in my piggy bank. Sometimes my Mom would give me a few pennies, nickels, dimes and/or quarters. My grandfather bought me a ceramic white with black polka dots piggy bank. I recall how excited I was to use it for my savings. There was a small hole at the bottom of the pig to release the change at an appointed time.

One day I had the idea to sell shells that I found at the neighborhood park. I charged twenty-five cents for three shells. All of that money went into my piggy bank as well. In the midst of most of the pennies that were in my bank I knew there were several quarters. The time came when I wanted to retrieve some of the money that was in my piggy bank. With my piggy bank in both hands, I shook it until a few coins fell out. A lot of pennies fell out, but I kept shaking the bank because I knew there were quarters inside.

There will be times when God places His hands on us, just as I had my hands on my piggy bank. He will shake us and some of our skills will come out. Yet, our God knows there are "quarters' (our gifts) inside of us. We go through trials and tribulations as we endure the shaking process. It is good to know that God knows our value, our worth because he put it inside of us. It wasn't until I shook out a dollar that I stopped shaking my piggy bank. God may have us go through a few things but the end result will show your true worth.

What trial(s) have you gone through that revealed your gift, talent or skill? How did you feel as you went through the "shaking process?"

The Eulogy

Be the Change God Wants You to Be

"Be transformed by the renewing of your mind…Romans 12:2"

What kind of person are you? Are you kind, caring, giving, selfish, determined, strong, easily influenced, loving, friendly, mean, tolerant, patient, hard-working, mindful, impatient, the list goes on and on. How do you see yourself? Do you ever wonder how people will see you when your final day on this earth comes? Did you make a difference in someone's life? Did you help when you saw someone in need and you were in a position to do something about it? Did you go on a fast on behalf of a friend or loved one who was so distraught over their situation that they needed someone to intercede for them?

If you could write your eulogy, what would you say? Would the things you write about reflect a person who was a servant for God or a servant of himself/herself? Were your resources used to gain advances in life at the expense of others, or were your resources used to help advance God's kingdom and His children?

We don't have to wait for the eulogy. We can make the changes right now. Each of us should examine our lives. If we took the time to review our everyday life, we would notice where change could be made.

So the question is, what will the dialogue of your eulogy have to say about you? You are in a position right now to be the change God wants you to be. Your eulogy doesn't have to be the end of your life. It can be the beginning of a new life. I challenge you to write your eulogy and watch a change take place in your life. Be honest and sincere with yourself as you write. As you come to the end of your message, you've actually started a new chapter in your life. How, you may ask? By listing what you have done. Now, go and conquer what you haven't done and make a difference. Be the change God wants you to be.

Shoes

Working in Your Gifts & Talents

"Each of you should use whatever gift you have received to serve others...1 Peter 4:10"

Shoes are a hot topic with some people. To them, it doesn't matter if we're talking about the latest gym shoes, the five-inch pumps, or a nice pair of boots. Selecting the right size shoe is key to comfort. I know some women, and men alike, who will sacrifice a shoe size for the look of the shoe because it goes with their outfit or it is a SHARP shoe. They are willing to walk in a shoe that does not fit so their shoes will match their outfit. The consequences are sore feet, blisters, corns and bunions. When their feet are exposed a person can see these signs of their pain.

Have you ever walked in the wrong shoe size of your gift and talents? Have you tried to be anything other than yourself? If so, you probably found yourself hurt, confused and frustrated. God has blessed each of us with gifts and talents. Too often we attempt to sing when our gift is cooking, or we try to draw when our gift is psychiatry. This doesn't mean we shouldn't explore new skills. We should be keenly aware of what fits us. When we do what we are made to do, we are able to perform naturally and it feels right. It doesn't cause us pain. We freely give and excel in our gifts when we own it.

A shoe salesperson may persuade you to buy a shoe because it is on sale. You have to decide, is it the right size? Do I need it? Can I afford it? Only you know your God given talent and gift because God has placed it in you. Don't let someone else determine your shoe size without you agreeing to it and checking it for yourself. As you walk in your gift you become more comfortable in it, just like wearing the right size pair of shoes. As you walk in them they become comfortable and fit perfectly.

Coffee Pot Manual

Reading the Instructions

"Study to show thyself approved unto God...2 Timothy 2:15"

Each morning my coffee pot generates coffee at 5:41am. When I purchased the coffee maker I read the instruction manual. I wanted to know how to operate every feature so I could get the maximum use from it. I set the programmer the night before, filled the filter with coffee grinds and the water reservoir with water. The blue light came on to indicate the programmer had been set. The next morning when I got up at 6:00am, my coffee was ready.

The Bible is our instruction manual for life. Reading the bible regularly and/or participating in bible study will help us to realize all that God has purposed for us. All too often, we don't know what the Word says about a situation so we handle it on our own without the guidance from God. God's Word does not discriminate. If we put the Word in action, it will produce results. If I didn't know how to program my coffee maker, I could still get my coffee, it just wouldn't be available when I got up. It's like knowing God's Word. We will still live in this world, but things could be easier. The Word of God speaks to every situation that we encounter.

    I forgot to set my coffee programmer one day and when I got up I was surprised to find that it wasn't made. Although it wasn't made I knew what I needed to do because I had read my manual. It was an easy fix. That evening I set the timer for the next morning. How often do we encounter problems and know how to handle them because the Word of God is in us? Most appliances, cars, and other items have manuals. To enjoy all that it has to offer we have to take time to read it. The Bible is no different. We have to take the time to read it.

Key to Ignition

Exercising your Faith

"And without faith it is impossible to please God...Hebrews 11:6"

If you believe in God for something, you must exercise your faith. God is moved when we believe that He will perform what we desire. It's not our job to understand the details, we just need faith. For those who drive cars, when you enter into your vehicle, you place the key in the ignition and your expectation is for the car to turn on. You are not concerned about the transmission, or the spark plugs, or the serpentine belt or any other detail of the engine. You have been conditioned that the vehicle will turn on when you turn the key.

Our faith in God is the same way. We trust that God has worked out all the details. Unless you are an auto mechanic or one who works on cars, to understand the functions of a car is a mystery.

There are so many wires, dipsticks, belts and other parts that cause a car to work. When our faith is exercised and we trust in God, we place ourselves in a position to not only receive for ourselves, but to help others as well. Once we place the key in the ignition and turn the car on, we are positioned to allow others to ride in the car with us. God has enough blessings for all of us. God may be using you to be the avenue for others to be blessed.

Exercise your faith! God's thoughts are complicated. We make situations difficult by trying to understand things that are over our heads. I've seen people try to start their cars and when it didn't start, they raised their hoods to examine the contents. The end result usually ended with the car being towed to a mechanic. Once the mechanic repaired the car it was ready to start and the owner's job was to put the key in the ignition. After your vehicle has been started, God may want to use you to be a blessing to others.

Student and the Teacher

Spiritual Partner

"Be not forgetful to entertain strangers: for thereby some have entertained angels unawares...Hebrews 13:2"

When a student is doing their work in class that a teacher has assigned to them and they understood the lesson, they usually don't ask questions. However, a teacher can tell if a student needs assistance by the perplexed look on a student's face. The teacher has grown accustomed to the student's ability as they spend time together in the classroom. The teacher has been assigned to oversee the student's academic work. It is the responsibility of the teacher to lead and guide. Nevertheless, the student has full access to the teacher to absorb as much knowledge as possible.

We are in a constant state of learning. God will provide us with a spiritual partner to guide us through our journey. While you are walking on your voyage of life, your spiritual partner may unexpectedly check on you when you need them the most. I've heard people say so many times, "I was going through and my friend called me just when I was about to break." That was an intentional call. Just as the teacher knows when the student needs assistance, your spiritual partner knows when you need a word of encouragement. Your spiritual partner will inspire you to continue when the road gets tough.

    Teachers want to see their students succeed. Teachers will provide resources and extra help to ensure their students understand the work. Our God is the same way. The spiritual partner he provides wants to see you succeed. As you move toward completing your assignment, it's important to remember God will never leave us nor forsake us to the very end.

Have you ever had someone to inspire/encourage you when you thought you were on a journey alone? Did you reach out to them once you knew they would support you on your assignment?

The Dandelion

Cutting the Root

"How often will my brother sin against me and I forgive him...Matthew 18:21"

Spring season brings about fresh flowers, pretty green grass and tweeting birds. I take delight in cutting grass. I like the smell of fresh cut grass. I like the feeling of walking on lush grass. I don't like the presence of the ever-growing bright yellow dandelions.

One sunny day, I mowed my lawn and got rid of all the yellow dandelions as I cut the grass, edged it, and blew away all of the grass clippings. The very next day I looked out my window and saw lots of bright yellow dandelions poking through the grass! I thought I mowed over them. How did they come back so soon?

It seems like this happens in our lives. How many times have you thought you forgave someone, or thought a situation was over only to find yourself talking about it again? How many times have you engaged in the same feelings wishing they would go away? How many times have you confessed that it's over but never got rid of the root?

I finally understood in order to get rid of the dandelions I had to cut the roots. Before the revelation, I was only cutting the top of the flower and admiring the beauty of everything around it. When I took the time to dig into the ground and uproot the root of the dandelion, I was able to get rid of the whole thing for good. I felt so good picking that first dandelion, but when I looked around my yard there were so many dandelions that I had to ask for help. I called a lawn company to spray my lawn to kill the roots.

We have to identify the root cause of our unforgiveness and be diligent about uprooting the roots. And, when we feel overwhelmed, just like when I called a lawn company to spray my lawn because it was too big a job for me to handle, we have to call on God and our spiritual partners to help us get through it.

Are you dealing with unforgiveness that you thought you dealt with? What actions did you take to rid yourself of the root of unforgiveness?

Heart Monitor

Trials and Tribulations

"Above all else, guard your heart, for everything you do flows from it...Proverbs 4:23"

I recently visited a dear friend in the hospital. As we were talking, I noticed the monitors she was hooked up to. There was a monitor that tracked the condition of her heart. The lines on the screen were bouncing up and down. The nurse came to check on my friend while I was there. She took her vital signs and gave her medicine as ordered by the doctor. I began to think, if those lines didn't go up and down the alternative would be a flat line. A flat line on a heart monitor signifies the absence of life.

In our lives we experience trials and tribulations as well as ups and downs. We have rainy and sunny days. I hear people saying I wish it were 85/90 degrees every day. The truth is, if it were those temperatures every day without some days of rain, our earth would dry up and fires would easily start. Just as, if it rained every day, our earth would risk floods. We need the rain as much as we need the sunshine. They work hand in hand. When we go through trials and tribulations we tend to get closer to God. We call on His Word, we pray to Him and we believe in God for deliverance. Those moments make us stronger in our faith. If everything were okay in our lives all the time, why would we call on God? How could we know God is a deliverer if we never needed Him to deliver us from anything? We need the trials and tribulations. We need the rain and the sunshine. We need God.

God's desire is to bring life and not just a regular life but an abundant life. During the rain we must remember that it is needed to make the grass grow, to wash our earth, to moisten the air and so many other crucial factors. Our trials and tribulations should encourage us to seek God and apply His word to our situation. As we advance out of this process we move into the sunshine. Then it's our time to enjoy life and share our testimonies.

Stepping Stone

Guidance in a Storm

"Christ Jesus himself is the chief cornerstone...Ephesians 2:20"

As I was listening to a dear friend speak about what she was going through, I was caught in a thought about stepping stones. Many people have goals in life, and they take a step each day to reach them. I'd like to think of taking steps on stepping stones. It's like going hiking and you are on a trail. As long as you stay on the stepping stone trail, you will reach the end of the trail and your destination. But what happens when a stepping stone is covered by debris, and you can't physically see where to take your next step. This is what many of us go through.

Our everyday life seems to be on track, when suddenly that "something" gets in the way. A child misbehaving, an unexpected bill that throws the budget off, a diagnosed sickness, etc. It can feel like a strong wind blowing everything into chaos, but we might need a strong wind to blow the debris out of the way so we can see where to take our next step. Those "somethings" come to make us stronger. If we don't look at them as troubles, but a strong wind to clear the debris, it all becomes part of the blessing.

Keep moving, keep pressing, and keep going. It's all a part of the process. The destination, your goal, is straight ahead. If your hiking partner complains that the winds are too strong and you need to go back, forge ahead. As the winds begin to settle, the path becomes clearer. Appreciate the challenges as they come so you can reach your goal and experience the blessing.

Seed

Spirit of Expectation

"Still other seed fell on good soil...Mark 4:8"

Gardening is one of my favorite hobbies. My grandparents had a large garden when I was a little girl. I would watch my grandfather till the dirt until it was smooth. He would place rich nutrients in the dirt to make it fertile. My grandmother would plant the seeds in the dirt.

Once their process was complete I had the pleasure of watering the seeds. I would tend to the seeds everyday while they were underground in the darkness. I'd ask my grandparents when the plants would come up. They were loving grandparents who had been gardening for years and knew the timing. They explained, in their terminology, the germination process. Although I didn't quite understand at the moment, I trusted what they told me.

A few weeks passed and I finally saw a green bud burst from the ground. With excitement I ran in the house and exclaimed, "We have plants!" I was ready to harvest it. My grandparents informed me the plants needed more time to mature before we could harvest it. Only then could we enjoy the bounty.

I couldn't see what was going on underground. My grandparents were experienced gardeners though. It came natural for them to encourage me to trust the process. As a family, one planted while the other nurtured. Before the green bud could burst through the dirt, it had to go through a transformation. As I watered it, it had a chance to grow because it was planted in fertile dirt.

We experience the same type of growth in our lives. We may have need of something. We go before God in prayer asking Him and by faith we believe that we will receive. As we place our trust in Him and wait on the process, in time, God delivers. We can't hurry God because His process is always on time and the right time. We can't always see during the dark moments what is going on, but God's germination process is at work.

Have you planted anything? What was your expectation?

Muscle up!
Strong Faith

"For while bodily training is of some value, godliness is of value in every way...1 Timothy 4:8"

When I go to the fitness center I find it intriguing to witness the muscle sizes of some patrons. I generally walk or run on the treadmill to get cardio exercise. As I glance around I tend to notice a few people who are lifting large amounts of weights. Sometimes they grunt out loud to get that last rep in. They look fatigued, but after a brief moment of rest, they are back at it again. I wonder, why does one continue to lift heavy weights? I see the strain, the sweat, the hard work and wonder is it worth it? Looking back on the muscle sizes of some patrons, I come to the conclusion that the more you work your muscle the more developed they become.

Faith works like our muscles. When we exercise our faith, our faith becomes stronger in God. We go through many reps of life, which can be exhausting. There are times when a person wants to quit, but you press on. You see the results of your faith and it inspires you to continue on your journey. God is our source of strength. I recall the size of the muscles on the fitness center patrons. I want my faith to be big, strong and mighty. I want my faith to carry me when I can't see my way. If we desire this type of faith, we have to put the work in. We will experience temptation and trials, but as we stay steady in faith, we will become stronger which will enable us to endure.

Can you recall a time when you felt like giving up? What encouraged you to keep going? Did you see your faith at work?

The Restaurant Cup

Getting Filled with the Fullness of God

"You prepare a table before me in the presence of my enemies; you anoint my head with oil; my cup overflows...Psalm 23:5"

When you go to a restaurant your "server" gladly takes your order, brings your food, and asks often if there's anything you need. But, there's something about the "cup". As you drink it, the server fills it up. You don't have to ask for a refill and no matter how much you drink, the server continues to fill the cup. It is the waiter/waitress' mission to supply you with everything you require in order to make your time in the restaurant as comfortable as possible. The more you require, the more you get. Their job is to make sure your cup is never empty.

This is our heavenly Father's philosophy as well. Ephesians 1:3 tell us that we have already been blessed with every spiritual blessing in Christ. All we need to do is receive. However, if we never pour out from the "cup", it can't be refilled. As we give (it's not always about money. We give our time, our talents, our compassion, etc.) HE continues to fill us up. Don't ever stop giving and doing well to others. It's a sure way to live an ABUNDANT life.

The Sun

God is Here

"He will never leave you nor forsake you...Deuteronomy 31:6"

    I recall flying to Tennessee on a cloudy, rainy day. The clouds were thick and the rain was heavy. The passengers and I began boarding the airplane. Once everyone had boarded and the flight attendants performed their normal preflight checks, we were on the runway preparing to take flight. I looked out the window and thought that it was such a gloomy day. It would be nice to travel on a sunny day.

    Soon, I heard the pilot say, "Flight attendants prepare for takeoff." As we sped down the runway, the rain hit the plane faster. We were soon ascending towards the clouds. Within a short time, we flew through the clouds. That's when I suddenly saw the sun. How could that be? It was cloudy and rainy on the ground. The higher we flew the less rain we encountered. It dawned on me the sun is ALWAYS shining. There are conditions that can block the sun, but the sun is always there.

We will have conditions in our life that will potentially block our faith in God. No matter how severe the condition is, God is ALWAYS here. As we place our mind on higher thoughts, we rise above our conditions. We will see God in every situation. Worry, a defeated mindset, and confusion can keep you in a low position. We might go through difficult times, just as the airplane flew through the clouds. The airplane kept flying and soon we saw the sun. If we keep pressing while reaching out to God, we will see the sun shining also.

When we remove obstacles out of our way, through prayer and belief, not only does the sun shine, but it also brings light to other dark places. Have you ever had a window open and it was cloudy outside? As soon as the clouds moved and the sun came out, the room was filled with light.

Often you can turn off the inside lights and use the sunlight. The sun provides many benefits when it enters a room. Our God provides unlimited benefits when He is in our lives.

Surge Protector

Overflow of Blessings

"For God gave us a spirit not of fear but of power and love and self-control...2 Timothy 1:7"

I have two surge protectors that I use for my business equipment. I use them to protect my electrical devices from voltage attacks. There have been times when my surge protector shut down. I knew that too much voltage was running through the lines. The surge protector did its job and as a result my equipment is still running problem free.

It's second nature to protect. A mother protects her child, a banker (tries to) protect a clients' money, and school administrators strive to protect their students. Each person in these examples will go to the extreme to protect. Their internal surge protector is designed to stop anyone from taking or hurting their prized possession. This is the way it should be.

I wonder how many of us have a surge protector on our blessings from God. How many times do we shut down before the overflow of blessings reach us? Just as a surge protector accommodates many outlets, we are equipped to receive many blessings. When we disconnect from the surge protector and hook into God's overflow we position ourselves to be abundantly blessed.

What makes us place a surge protector on our life? Fear! That fear shows up as a fear of the unknown, a fear of failure, or a fear of success. When we replace fear with faith we disconnect the surge protector.

We are the Writers; God is the Editor

Writers and editors have a very close relationship. The writer comes up with ideas and stories and tries to get down everything they imagine in their mind. The editor comes along later to make changes, rearrange things and fix mistakes in the writing. The writer and editor will need to work closely together to make sure the writer's message is coming across to the readers in the best way possible.

Just as the writer/editor relationship is very close, so should our relationship be with God. We may plan our lives and structure things in the way we would like for them to be, but God has His view of our lives. When we examine our lives we can often see His way of editing our story (life).

For example, there may be times we have a conversation with someone. After we leave the conversation, we may feel a tug inside. When we open our hearts to God by asking Him what that tug is about, He will reveal to us His edit. Sometimes He may tell us that we were not showing that person His love in the way we communicated with them. Sometimes, He wants to let us know how we can further help that person in a practical way. We can always ask God His view on our conversations and activities knowing that He will answer.

I am free to write, because God is the perfect editor.

Made in the USA
Coppell, TX
28 January 2021

49009229R00069